Future You Is Watching

What Most People Learn Too Late

Kash Middleton

ISBN: 979-8-9955546-0-8

Published independently in the United States of America

For your future self.

Leo was fifteen.

He didn't like asking for money.

He wanted something of his own.

But not just money.

Something that was his.

He wrote down a few ideas.

Dog walking.
Car washing.
Mowing lawns.

They were fine ideas.

He tried a few.

They just never stuck.

Dog walking
Car washing
Mowing lawns

One afternoon, he noticed something.

On hot days, people slowed down.

They looked for shade.
And something cold.

Not one person.

A lot of them.

For the first time,

he wasn't trying to think of an idea.

He was seeing one.

He started small.

A folding table.
A simple sign.
Fresh lemonade.

LEMONADE
$2

Customers gathered.

He squeezed every lemon by hand.

His hands worked faster than they ever had.

Still, it wasn't fast enough.

EMONADE $2

The line moved slowly.

By the end of the day,
a few stepped away.

$2 Lemonade

A customer noticed the line thinning.

“You’d move faster with a machine,” he said.

Leo kept squeezing and gave a small nod.

He didn’t run out of customers.

He ran out of time.

That night, he counted his money.

It was more than he expected.

He stared at the total.

$2
LEMONAD

Later, he opened another tab.

The sneakers he'd been looking at were still there.

On sale.

He had enough saved.

If he tapped “buy,”
they’d be on his doorstep in two days.

No one would blame him.
He earned it.

His thumb hovered.

20% OFF
$79.99
20% OFF!
Add to Cart

Then that customer's voice followed.

"You'd move faster with a machine."

$2 Lemonade

He stared at what he'd made.

Switched tabs.

Typed: juicers.

He compared prices.

Then looked at the sneakers.

Still on sale.

Then back to the juicers.

20% OFF
Add to Cart

He couldn’t buy both.

Not yet.

He closed the tab.

Two days passed.

A box arrived.

He opened it.

Inside was the machine.

He brought it to the stand.

The first cup filled in seconds.

$2 Lemona

He had time to breathe.

The line moved faster.

No one stepped out.

$2 Lemonade

“Do you have apple juice?” someone asked.

Leo shook his head.

“Not yet,” he said.

“I’d buy that,” another voice said.

Leo made a note.

apple juice

The next week,
there was something new on the table.

Apple.

It didn’t replace lemonade.
It joined it.

By the end of the day,
it was gone.

Lemonade
Apple

The week after that,
there were three options.

Lemon.
Apple.
Watermelon.

He didn't wait to be asked.

The cups felt temporary.

Some customers asked if they could take it to go.

So he tried something sturdier.

Bottles.

Sealed and easy to carry.

But the bottles looked plain.

That night,
he opened his laptop.

Not to scroll.
Not to play.

He typed two words.

Next Juice.

Next Juice

He tried a few versions.

Deleted them.
Tried again.

He closed the screen.

Next Juice

The bottles didn't stay plain for long.

A small label appeared.

Next Juice.

Simple.
Clean.

Customers started saying it.

"Is this Next Juice?"
He nodded.

NEXT
JUICE
NEXT
JUICE
NEXT
JUICE
NEXT
JUICE
NEXT
JUICE

The folding table became two.
Then three.

One morning,
a banner stretched across the tables.

Next Juice.

Next Juice

He stepped back.

For the first time,
it felt like something that was his.

He saw how one decision had changed his direction.

The line stretched past the corner.

NEXT
NEXT JUIC
Citruis Jiucees

After packing up for the day,
he paused.

The tables folded.
The banner rolled.

The sidewalk grew quiet again.

Citrus Juicer
each pour
easy pour
pulp filter
pulp filter

He thought about the first upgrade.

The machine.

How small it felt when it arrived.

How much it changed things.

Citrus Juicer

He remembered the sneakers.

Still on sale.

This time,
the price didn't feel heavy.

Paid for in an afternoon.

Citrus Juicer
Thank You
For Your Purchase
$79.99

The difference wasn't the sneakers.

It was the timing.

Future you is watching.

Kash Middleton believes that small decisions made today shape the life we live tomorrow.

His mission is to inspire readers to think ahead and make choices that their future self will be proud of.

Future You Is Watching was created to help readers understand the importance of patience, discipline, and thoughtful choices—one decision at a time.

Every decision you make today
is building your future.

What choice will you make
knowing that your future is watching?

www.ingramcontent.com/pod-product-compliance
Lightning Source LLC
LaVergne TN
LVHW070218110826
845147LV00003B/603

* 9 7 9 8 9 9 5 5 5 4 6 0 8 *